CW00859771

Sunshine Wallace

Estes Park, Colorado

Estes Park is one of the most beautiful cities in the United States. A couple of the things that make it beautiful is Fall River and the wildlife that make their homes here. The trout filled river attracts fisherman as well as black bears. Rocky Mountain elk wander around, most often found on the golf course, grazing on grass or stopping cars by standing in the road for no reason. Bighorn sheep and mountain goats are frequently spotted climbing up and down the walls of the canyon if you're headed out of Estes towards Loveland. They are certainly something to see! You'll most likely not gaze upon a mountain lion or moose, but you never know! There is a lot to do in this sweet little town. Taking a walk through downtown on the Riverwalk and popping into the local candy shops or grabbing some food at one of the many restaurants. The free concerts at Performance Park from June through August are fun! Ohhhh! The Stanley Hotel is famous for a visit from scary book author, Stephen King. He was so inspired by the hotel that he wrote a book called *The Shining*, which scares the pants off anyone who reads it or watches the movie. The Stanley has many choices of restaurants and activities like ghost tours and magic shows. Open-air Adventure Park and the Aerial Tram are fun for everyone. Fishing, rafting, hiking, ATV tours are all available from local businesses. And of course, the Rocky Mountain National Park is a must see and the entrance to the park is in Estes Park.

Some activities are seasonal

FOR ALL THE KIDS ON FALL RIVER

ESPECIALLY
PAYTEN, AVERY, LEVI, ROWAN,
KORA, THE ANGEL ON THE WAY,
& THE BEST PUPPY RIVER

YOU ARE UNIQUE.
YOU ARE KIND.
YOU DESERVE TO BE
HAPPY!

Bighorn Sheep

Yellow-bellied Marmot

Mountain Goat

Rocky Mountain Elk

Mule Deer

Beaver

Black Bear

Moose

Mountain Lion

Pika

River Otter

Magpie

Sorry not Sorry!

You don't have to say you're sorry for being yourself.
Don't apologize for the way you
laugh or
dress or
talk or
smile or
your sense of humor or
what makes you happy!
Being yourself is the best way to be.

BIGHORN
SHEEP

OHHH! BIGHORN SHEEP ARE NOT THE FUZZY LOOKIN' ANIMALS ON OLD MCDONALD'S FARM. THESE GUYS ARE BEASTS! THE MALES, ALSO KNOWN AS RAMS, HAVE LARGE, CURLED HORNS THAT WEIGH UP TO 30 POUNDS AND GROW UP TO 45 INCHES LONG. IMAGINE PUTTING AN OBJECT THAT WEIGHS 30 POUNDS ON YOUR HEAD AND THEN WALK UP THE SIDE OF A MOUNTAIN ... YOU'RE KIDDING, RIGHT? NOT A FEAT FOR US HUMANS! THE FEMALES, CALLED EWES, ARE A BIT SMALLER AND THEIR HORNS AREN'T AS BIG. BIGHORN SHEEP HAVE SPLIT HOOVES THAT ARE ROUGH AND COVER UP A SOFT PAD THAT CONFORMS TO THE ROCKS TO HELP THEM GRIP SMALL LEDGES. BIGHORN SHEEP HAVE BEAUTIFUL, BIG EYES THAT ARE POSITIONED WIDELY APART TO HELP THEM VIEW AND NAVIGATE THEIR WORLD SAFELY. WOLVES, MOUNTAIN LIONS, GOLDEN EAGLES, AND COYOTES HUNT NEWBORN SHEEP FOR FOOD SO THE EWES GIVE BIRTH UP HIGH ON THE MOUNTAIN. BET THOSE GOLDEN EAGLES CAUSE THOSE MAMA SHEEP TROUBLE WAY UP HIGH WHILE THE OTHERS ARE DOWN ON THE GROUND, LICKING THEIR CHOPS.

BIGHORN SHEEP

THE ONLY PERSON YOU
NEED TO BE BETTER THAN
IS THE PERSON YOU WERE
YESTERDAY.

I am me
Just how I want to be
And all I need
To be me
Is to
Faithfully
And happily
Agree
To be
Free to believe
That
Being me means
Skinny me
Chubby me
Cuddly me
Happy me
Angry me
Nervous me
Confused me
Scared me
is
Magically
Perfectly
Beautifully
ME!
The me that has big dreams
And likes feeling special
And wants to be seen
And I believe
You should be
Seen, too

YELLOW-BELLIED
MARMOT

THE YELLOW-BELLIED MARMOT IS A CUTE LITTLE RODENT WITH A FEW COOL NICKNAMES ... ONE BEING THE ROCK CHUCK AND I CAN'T GET OVER HOW CUTE THAT SOUNDS! ALSO KNOWN AS A GROUND SQUIRREL AND WHISTLE PIG, THE YELLOW BELLIED MARMOT IS AN INTERESTING LITTLE GUY. THEIR FUR IS MAINLY BROWN, WITH A DARK BUSHY TAIL, YELLOW CHEST AND WHITE PATCH BETWEEN THE EYES, AND THEY WEIGH UP TO 11 POUNDS. THEY LIVE IN BURROWS IN COLONIES OF UP TO 20 CREATURES WITH A SINGLE DOMINANT MALE. THEY EAT PLANTS, INSECTS, AND BIRD EGGS. ROCK CHUCKS HIBERNATE IN SEPTEMBER AND IT LASTS THROUGH THE WINTER. EACH MALE MARMOT DIGS A BURROW SOON AFTER IT WAKES FROM HIBERNATION, AND STARTS LOOKING FOR FEMALES TO EXPAND THEIR COLONIES. BY SUMMER, IT MAY HAVE UP TO FOUR FEMALE MATES. YELLOW-BELLIED MARMOTS SPEND ABOUT 80% OF THEIR LIVES IN THEIR BURROWS, 60% OF WHICH IS SPENT HIBERNATION. THEY OFTEN SPEND MID-DAY AND NIGHT IN A BURROW AS WELL. THESE BURROWS ARE USUALLY CONSTRUCTED ON A SLOPE, SUCH AS A HILL, MOUNTAIN, OR CLIFF. THEY DIG THEIR BURROWS UNDER ROCKS TO BE SAFER FROM PREDATORS LIKE FOXES, DOGS, COYOTES, WOLVES, AND EAGLES. UPON SEEING A PREDATOR, THE YELLOW-BELLIED MARMOT WHISTLES TO WARN THE OTHERS IN THE AREA, AFTER WHICH IT TYPICALLY HIDES IN A NEARBY ROCK PILE UNTIL THERE IS NO MORE THREAT. YELLOW-BELLIED MARMOTS DO NOT HAVE GREAT EYESIGHT BUT IT HAS EXCELLENT SENSE OF SMELL AND HEARING.

YELLOW-BELLIED MARMOT

Things to Remember

Other people's opinion of you has nothing to do with you.

Every struggle is a step in the right direction.

Mistakes are a part of growing.

Worrying changes nothing.

The best you can do is not give up.

Negative thinking keeps you from what you deserve.

INNER CRITIC

Your inner critic is that voice that speaks to you negatively about who you are as a human. It makes you think there is something terribly wrong with you when there is nothing wrong with you. This voices only goal is to make you believe in the very worst of yourself and when you start thinking positively, it tries to bring you back down. It grows stronger the more you listen to it without having ways of silencing it. One way to help yourself learn to recognize when that critic is bringing you down is to give it a name. I named mine Broccoli. Broccoli likes to tell me things like I'm not smart enough or I don't belong. It likes to make me feel bad by telling me how annoying I am and how everyone thinks so, too. Broccoli tells me I should keep to myself. That I am unlovable, and that I am weird. Broccoli even whispers how annoying I am when I talk and that my laugh is too loud. It tells me I should dress like everyone around me instead of dressing how I please. Broccoli tries to convince me that how I feel, think, or say doesn't matter. The things in life that bring me joy aren't worth seeking because I'm not worth feeling joy. My inner critic tries to convince me that my successes are not anything special and neither am I. Broccoli wants me to believe that everyone around me is tired of me and that life would be better if I would stay away.

None of this is true. NONE. OF. IT.

If Broccoli were real, I'd dip it in ranch and chew it up. I'd then probably spit it out because ...

I DO NOT LIKE BROCCOLI!

MOUNTAIN
GOAT

THE MOUNTAIN GOAT IS A LARGE MAMMAL COVERED WITH LONG WHITE FUR OR WOOL. THEY SHED THEIR THICK FUR IN THE WARMER MONTHS BY RUBBING UP AGAINST TREES. THEY DO LOOK FUNNY WHEN ONLY BITS OF THEIR FUR IS MISSING. THEIR COAT MATCHES THE SNOW AND KEEPS IT HIDDEN FROM PREDATORS LIKE COUGARS, LYNXES, WOLVERINES, BEARS, GOLDEN EAGLES, TO NAME A FEW. COUGARS ARE THEIR BIGGEST THREAT BECAUSE THEY TOO ARE GREAT AT NAVIGATING THEIR WAY AROUND A MOUNTAIN. THEY GROW UP TO 3 FEET AND WEIGH UP TO 180 POUNDS. THESE BIG GOATS HAVE BLACK LIPS, NOSTRILS, HOOVES, AND HORNS. THEIR HOOVES ARE LIKE THE MOUNTAIN SHEEP, HARD SHELLS ON TOP OF A SOFT PAD THAT HELPS THEM WALK ON THE SIDE OF MOUNTAINS AND OVER ROCKS EASILY. ADULTS HAVE LONG HAIR UNDER THEIR THROATS THAT LOOKS LIKE A BEARD. BOTH MALES AND FEMALES HAVE SHARP POINTED HORNS THAT CURVE SLIGHTLY BACKWARD. THE MALE GOAT IS CALLED A BILLY AND THE FEMALE IS CALLED A NANNY. THEIR KIDS, WELL, THEY'RE CALLED KIDS. MOUNTAIN GOATS GRAZE ON GRASSES, SHRUBS, CONIFERS, AND FORBS IN SUMMER.

MOUNTAIN GOAT

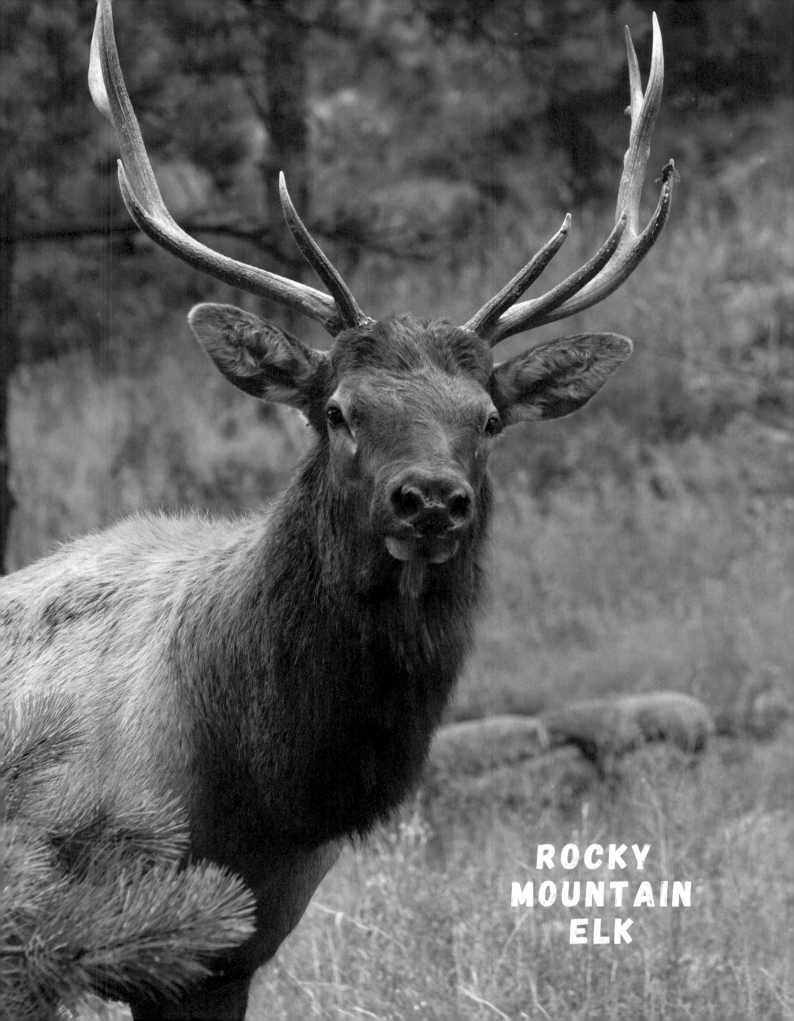

ROCKY
MOUNTAIN
ELK

ROCKY MOUNTAIN ELK ARE FOUND IN THE ROCKY MOUNTAINS AND ADJACENT AREAS OF WESTERN NORTH AMERICA. THESE ARE MAGNIFICENT SHOWSTOPPERS OF ANIMALS. THEY HAVE THE LARGEST ANTLERS OF ALL SUBSPECIES. THEY WEIGH UP TO 40 POUNDS. THEIR ANTLERS GROW SO QUICKLY, UP TO AN INCH A DAY, THAT SCIENTISTS ARE STUDYING THEM TO HELP FIND A CURE FOR CANCER. AMAZING! THEY ARE MOST OFTEN FOUND IN FOREST AND FOREST EDGE HABITATS AND IN MOUNTAIN REGIONS WHERE THEY OFTEN STAY IN HIGHER ELEVATIONS DURING WARMER MONTHS AND COME DOWN LOWER IN THE WINTER. LISTEN FOR THEM! THEY'RE NOISY! THE MALES, CALLED BULLS, MAKE AN UNREAL SOUND CALLED BUGLING. IT'S A HIGH-PITCH SOUND THAT IS THE COMBINATION OF A ROAR AND WHISTLE AND, BELIEVE ME, YOU'LL BE SHOCKED THE FIRST TIME YOU HEAR IT. FROM EARLY SEPTEMBER THROUGH OCTOBER, BULLS CAN BE HEARD BUGLING AT TWILIGHT. THIS SOUND IS MADE TO SHOW OFF FOR THE FEMALES, CALLED COWS, AND TO LET OTHER BULLS KNOW THEY MEAN BUSINESS. THE FIRST TIME I HEARD AN ELK BUGLE, IT SCARED ME SO BEWARE! ALSO, LISTEN FOR CLICKING SOUNDS. THEIR ANKLES CLICK TO LET THE OTHER ELK AHEAD OF THEM KNOW IT'S AN ELK BEHIND THEM AND NOT A PREDATOR. THESE STALLIONS WITH ANTLERS ARE MY FAVORITE WILD ANIMALS ON FALL RIVER.

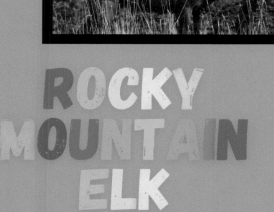

ROCKY
MOUNTAIN
ELK

THE WORST YOU CAN DO IS TO STOP TRYING!

What is brave?

Ready to face fear, showing courage.

Asking for help

Standing up for yourself

Apologizing

Challenging yourself

Trying new things

Talking about your problems

Speaking up

Doing the right thing

Meeting new people

Dreaming big

Being yourself

Saying no

Not following the crowd

Sunshine's List of me

I love how I laugh

I like bananas

I don't like mean people

I like my nails painted

I don't like cold weather

I love when the day is about to
turn into night

I don't like tomatoes

I love to read

I love animals so much!

I don't like green veggies

I like the color blue

I love spending time by myself

I love teaching people about animals

Your List of me

Your turn! Make a list of the things you love, like, and don't like. It's all you and you are wonderful! Don't ever forget it!

MULE DEER

THE MULE DEER ARE OFTEN CALLED DEER OF THE WEST. BLACK-TAILED DEER OR BURRO DEER. WITH ITS BIG EARS (THEY RESEMBLE A MULE'S EARS AND THAT'S HOW THEY GOT THEIR NAME!), BROWN-GRAY COATS WITH CREAM AND WHITE-COLORED RUMPS. THEIR LITTLE TAILS ARE WHITE WITH A TUFT OF BLACK HAIRS AT THE TIP. THEY WEIGH UP TO 330 POUNDS AND STAND AROUND 3 FEET AT THE SHOULDERS. THESE GUYS, LIKE THEIR COUSINS, THE WHITE-TAILED DEER, ARE HERBIVORES, WHICH MEANS THEY EAT PLANTS, NUTS, CORN, TREES, AND TWIGS. THESE GUYS DON'T RUN LIKE THEIR COUSINS BUT LEAP OVER DISTANCES UP TO 8 YARDS AND CAN REACH SPEEDS UP TO 45 MILES AN HOUR. THEIR ANTLERS FORK AS THEY QUICKLY GROW INSTEAD OF LIKE THEIR COUSINS THAT BRANCH OUT FROM A SINGLE MAIN BEAM. EACH SPRING, A BUCK SHEDS ITS ANTLERS AND A NEW SET QUICKLY STARTS TO REPLACE THE OLD PAIR.

MULE
DEER

THERE IS ALWAYS, ALWAYS, ALWAYS SOMETHING TO BE GRATEFUL FOR.

IT'S OKAY

⭐ To make a mistake

⭐ To have bad days

⭐ To be less than perfect

⭐ To do what's best for you

⭐ To be yourself

⭐ To stand up for yourself

Sunshine Tea

4 CUPS OF WATER

5 TEA BAGS

CLEAR, GLASS PITCHER

WITH LID

PUT TEA BAGS & WATER INTO THE PITCHER. PUT IN THE SUN FOR 4 HOURS. SERVE!

Sunshine Strawberry Lemonade

4 CUPS OF WATER

2 TBSP OF SWEETENER

3 TEA BAGS

1 LEMON, SLICED

4-6 LARGE STRAWBERRIES, TOPS REMOVED, SLICED IN HALF

CONTAINER WITH LID

COMBINE WATER & SWEETENER ADD TEA BAGS & FRUIT. PUT IN SUN FOR 2 HOURS. SERVE!

BEAVER

WHEN I WAS YOUNG, I WAS TEASED ABOUT MY TEETH. UNTIL I GOT MY BRACES, KIDS CALLED ME BUCKY BEAVER AND THAT WAS NOT A GOOD TIME FOR ME. I LEARNED FROM BEING PICKED ON FOR SOMETHING I COULDN'T HELP, THOUGH. I LEARNED THAT TEASING AND CALLING PEOPLE UGLY NAMES FOR LAUGHS HURTS. THAT'S WHY I THRIVE ON KINDNESS INSTEAD OF MEANNESS. NOW, HERE'S THE STORY OF THE REAL BEAVERS, THE LARGEST RODENT IN NORTH AMERICA. THEY ARE SOCIAL ANIMALS AND LIVE IN GROUPS OF UP TO 8 CALLED COLONIES. THEY BUILD DAMS OR LODGES WITH THE NATURAL MATERIALS THEY GATHER SUCH AS STICKS, REEDS, BRANCHES, SAPLINGS, MUD, AND ROCKS. BY DOING THIS, BEAVERS ARE ABLE TO MAKE NEW HABITATS FOR THE AQUATIC LIFE AROUND THEM AS WELL AS BUILD THEMSELVES A LODGE FOR SLEEPING. THEY USE THEIR LARGE FRONT TEETH, WHICH ARE COLORED ORANGE, TO CHEW THROUGH AND CARRY THEIR SUPPLIES TO BUILD THEIR DAMS. THEIR DAMS HAVE MANY ENTRANCES WITH THEIR SLEEPING AREA ABOVE WATER. BEAVERS COMMUNICATE WITH EACH OTHER WITH SOUNDS LIKE GRUNTS, GRUMBLES, AND BARKS, WITH SCENTS, AND TAIL SLAPPING. TAIL SLAPPING IS USED AS AN ALARM SYSTEM TO WARN OTHERS OF DANGER.

BEAVER

Empathy

In the boxes, describe ways you can show and practice empathy for others

How To Stay True To Yourself

Four necessary tips that help you be you.

1 Check yourself! Be mindful about how you feel inside with what you want and need. Checking in with your body and being honest with yourself about how you're feeling will guide you in the right direction. If it feels wrong, don't act until you feel right.

2 Choose your friends wisely! Surround yourself with good people. People that tell you the truth, that love you, that respect you, that actually see the amazing person you are!

3 Remember, sometimes no matter what you do, how you act, or if you have the best of intentions, not everyone will like you. Learn to be ok with that uneasy feeling because if you let people bring you down, it can hurt your sweet heart. Be you!

4 Learn to admit you're wrong when you know you're wrong and right any wrong you may have committed as soon as you notice. This way your conscious can rest and you can look yourself in the eye and say you did the right thing at the right time. The right time is up to you and how you want to handle the situation. Just because you're wrong does not mean you are bad. It means you're human.

Stand up for what is right.

Do it thoughtfully
Do it kindly
Stay true to yourself

THE WORST YOU CAN DO IS TO STOP TRYING!

Solo Chicken Quesadilla

Ingredients

1/3 cup pre-cooked chicken, chopped
1 tsp taco seasoning
2 Flour tortillas
Shredded cheese
Optional:
Sour Cream
Salsa
Pico
Cilantro

Always have an adult present.

Instructions

Spray skillet with cooking spray and pre-heat on medium for a few minutes. Place one tortilla on pan. Layer a small amount of cheese, leaving about 1/4 inch bare around the edge of tortilla. Spread chicken over cheese. Add another thin layer of cheese on top of chicken and top with tortilla. Cook until tortilla is light brown. Carefully flip and cook until light brown. Place on cutting board and cut into fourths. Serve with salsa, sour cream, pico. Garnish with cilantro.

BLACK
BEAR

BLACK BEARS FOUND AROUND FALL RIVER ARE LIKE BIG RACCOONS! THEY'RE A NUISANCE FOR RESIDENTS BECAUSE THEY GET IN TRASH CANS LOOKING FOR FOOD JUST LIKE THE TRASH BANDITS KNOWN AS RACCOONS. BLACK BEARS LOVE FISH SO THEY CAN SOMETIMES BE FOUND FISHING TROUT IN THE RIVER. THEY ARE OMNIVORES WHICH MEANS THEY EAT FRUITS, BERRIES, INSECTS, EGGS, FISH, HONEY, AND SOMETIMES EVEN YOUNG DEER, MOOSE, ELK, AND SHEEP. BLACK BEARS BARK! THEY CAN RUN UP TO 30 MILES AN HOUR AND CAN CLIMB TREES AND SWIM. THEIR FUR IS THICK, WITH MANY LAYERS OF SHAGGY HAIR THAT KEEPS THEM WARM DURING THE COLD WINTER MONTHS. THEY'RE CALLED BLACK BEARS BUT THEY'RE NOT ALWAYS BLACK. SOME BEARS COME IN RED, BROWN OR EVEN WHITE. THEY SPEND THE COLD MONTHS HIBERNATING IN CAVES OR DENS. THE MAMA BEAR HAS HER BABIES IN THE DENS AND SPEND THE NEXT SEVERAL MONTHS CARING AND LOVING ON THEM. THE BLACK BEAR IS SMALLER THAN THE GRIZZLY BEAR, WEIGHING IN AT THE MOST, 250 POUNDS. NORMALLY, BLACK BEARS FEAR HUMANS BUT IF HUMANS FEED THEM, THEY BECOME AGGRESSIVE AND WILL ATTACK TO GET FOOD. THEY'RE CUTE BUT DEADLY SO WATCH FOR THEM DURING THE WARM MONTHS.

**BLACK
BEAR**

Today I am grateful for ...

01 ....
02 ....
03 ....
04 ....
05 ....
06 ....
07 ....
08 ....
09 ....
10 ....
11 ....
12 ....
13 ....
14 ....
15 ....

16 ....
17 ....
18 ....
19 ....
20 ....
21 ....
22 ....
23 ....
24 ....
25 ....
26 ....
27 ....
28 ....
29 ....
30 ....

Ohhh! You're good!

MOOSE

MOOSE ARE HUGE! THEY ARE THE LARGEST MEMBERS OF THE DEER FAMILY AND THE LARGEST LAND MAMMAL IN NORTH AMERICA. THEY CAN WEIGH MORE THAN 1,300 POUNDS AND GET AS TALL AS 8 FEET WITH ANTLERS 6 FEET WIDE. THESE ARE BEASTS!! MALES, CALLED BULLS, ONLY GROW ANTLERS, NOT THE FEMALES, CALLED COWS. MOOSE BABIES ARE CALLED CALVES AND THEY STAY WITH THEIR MOTHERS UNTIL THEY ARE GROWN. THEY LIVE IN COLD AREAS BECAUSE THEIR BIG BODIES DO NOT ADJUST WELL TO HOT WEATHER. THEY EAT GRASS, SHRUBS, BARK, AND PINECONES. MOOSE LOVE TO SWIM AND CAN SWIM FOR MILES AND MILES AND STAY UNDERWATER FOR UP TO HALF A MINUTE. THEY'VE BEEN SEEN PLAYING IN WATER WHICH WOULD BE SO COOL TO SEE! IN THE SPRING, MOOSE HUNT FOR FOOD IN RIVERS AND LAKES. THEY LOOK FOR TALL GRASS BECAUSE THEY CANNOT BEND OVER VERY FAR. THEY CAN RUN FAST, REACHING UP TO 35 MILES AN HOUR. MOOSE HAVE EXCELLENT HEARING AND A FANTASTIC SENSE OF SMELL. THESE SUPER SENSES MAKE UP FOR THEIR POOR EYESIGHT.

MOOSE

Standing by a tree
Just wasting my time
when along came some
little people no larger
than dimes. The king
came up and asked me
my name.
"My name is Ted and stomping
is my game. So why don't
you go and leave me alone!
March back to your castle and sit
on your throne."
That king got mad and started
yelling at me so I raised up
my foot and tried to squash
them like fleas
Ten minutes later I still had nothing
to do until I looked beside me
and saw a big ol' shoe. "You scared
the little people!"
Is what the giant said.
So he raised up his foot, "Ha Ha!
Now you're dead!"

YOU MATTER!
YOU MEAN SOMETHING!
YOU ARE SEEN!

Cinnamon Roll Smoothie

1 CUP MILK
1 ½ FROZEN BANANAS, CUT INTO CHUNKS
¼ TEASPOON CINNAMON
½ TEASPOON VANILLA EXTRACT
1 TSP BROWN SUGAR, OPTIONAL
⅓ CUP OLD-FASHIONED OATS
1 CUP ICE
BLEND TILL SMOOTH

Smoothest Smoothie

3/4 CUP PLAIN YOGURT
1/2 CUP 100% PURE FRUIT JUICE
1 1/2 CUPS (6 1/2 OUNCES) FROZEN
FRUIT, SUCH AS BLUEBERRIES,
RASPBERRIES, PINEAPPLE OR
PEACHES
BLEND TILL SMOOTH

Always have an adult present.

MOUNTAIN
LION

MOUNTAIN LIONS ARE KNOWN BY MANY NAMES: PUMA, COUGAR, CATAMOUNT, OR PANTHER. IT'S THE LARGEST SPECIES OF WILD CAT IN NORTH AMERICA AND THE FOURTH LARGEST CAT IN THE WORLD. THEY CAN GROW TO 3 FEET TALL AND 8 FEET LONG! THEY HAVE A BEAUTIFUL, SLEEK, TAWNY-COLORED COAT. FEMALES ARE SMALLER THAN MALES WEIGHING AROUND 110 POUNDS WHILE THE MALE CAN REACH UP TO 180 POUNDS. THEY LOOK VERY SIMILAR TO THE HOUSE CAT, AND THEY CANNOT ROAR SO THEY ARE NOT CONSIDERED PART OF THE BIG CAT GROUP LIKE AFRICAN LIONS AND ASIAN TIGERS. THEY HAVE ROUND HEADS, POWERFUL JAWS AND RETRACTABLE CLAWS. BABIES ARE NORMALLY SPOTTED WITH RINGS AROUND THEIR TAILS. COUGARS ARE SHY AND BRAVE. THEY HUNT ANIMALS MUCH LARGER THAN THEMSELVES LIKE MOOSE AND ELK. THEY ARE FAMOUS FOR THEIR SNEAK ATTACKS BY LURKING BEHIND, NOT CHASING THEIR PREY, AND AMBUSHING THEM UNEXPECTEDLY. IF YOU COME ACROSS A MOUNTAIN LION, ACT LIKE A GRIZZLY AND ROAR, MAKE YOURSELF LOOK BIGGER BY PUTTING YOUR ARMS ABOVE YOUR HEAD, MAKE EYE CONTACT, AND DON'T RUN! STAND YOUR GROUND!

MOUNTAIN
LION

DON'T BE AFRAID OF WHAT COULD GO WRONG. GET EXCITED ABOUT THE THINGS THAT WILL GO RIGHT!!

SCAVENGER HUNT

MARK OFF EACH WORD WHEN YOU FIND IT

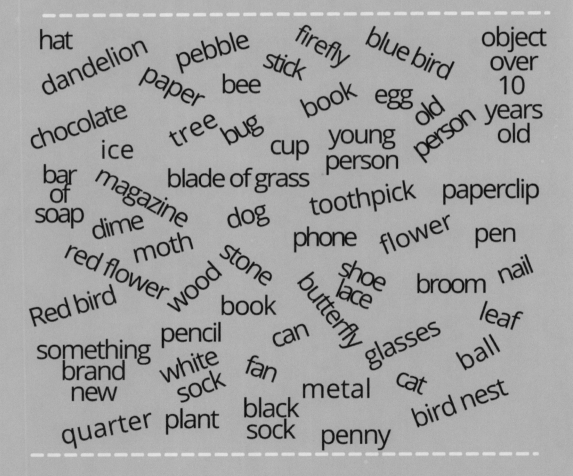

hat
dandelion
pebble
firefly
blue bird
object over 10 years old
chocolate
paper
bee
stick
book
egg
old person
ice
tree
bug
cup
young person
bar of soap
magazine
blade of grass
toothpick
paperclip
dime
dog
phone
flower
pen
red flower
moth
wood
stone
shoe lace
broom
nail
Red bird
book
butterfly
glasses
leaf
something brand new
pencil
white sock
can
fan
metal
cat
ball
quarter
plant
black sock
penny
bird nest

MANGO PEACH SMOOTHIE

1 ½ CUPS MILK

1 CUP DICED PEACHES

1 CUP CHOPPED MANGO

½ TEASPOON VANILLA EXTRACT

1 CUP ICE

BLEND TILL SMOOTH

CHOCOLATE PEANUT BUTTER BANANA SMOOTHIE

1 FROZEN BANANA

1 CUP MILK

¼ CUP OLD-FASHIONED ROLLED OATS

3 TABLESPOONS PEANUT BUTTER

1 TABLESPOON COCOA POWDER

A FEW CHOCOLATE CHIPS

BLEND TILL SMOOTH

ALWAYS HAVE AN ADULT PRESENT.

PIKA

PIKAS ARE SMALL MAMMALS THAT ARE CLOSELY RELATED TO RABBITS AND HARES BUT RESEMBLE CHINCHILLAS. THEY HAVE SHORT LIMBS AND ROUND BODIES, WITH NO TAILS. PIKAS ARE ALSO KNOWN AS ROCK RABBITS. THEY LIVE ON ROCKY MOUNTAINSIDES, WHERE THERE ARE NUMEROUS TINY AREAS WHERE THEY CAN SEEK SHELTER. PIKAS REQUIRE COLD TEMPERATURES TO LIVE AND CAN DIE IF EXPOSED TO TEMPERATURES ABOVE 77.9 °F. CHANGING TEMPERATURES HAVE FORCED SOME PIKA POPULATIONS TO MOVE TO EVEN HIGHER ELEVATIONS. THEY ARE HERBIVORES AND EAT GRASS, FIREWEED, MOSS, LICHEN, AND SHRUB TWIGS. THEY LIVE IN GROUPS CALLED COLONIES. IF IN DANGER OR SCARED, THEY BARK TO WARN OTHER PIKAS SOMETHING BAD IS ABOUT TO GO DOWN. THEY ARE MOST ACTIVE DURING THE DAY. DURING THE MATING SEASON, THEY SING SONGS WITH EACH OTHER, TO ATTRACT THE OPPOSITE SEX. FEMALE PIKAS GIVE BIRTH TO UP TO 5 BABIES. THEIR BABIES GROW UP VERY QUICKLY AND LEAVE THEIR MOMS AROUND 3 MONTHS OLD.

PIKA

IF YOU DON'T GO AFTER WHAT YOU WANT, YOU WILL NEVER HAVE IT.

Things to do in Estes Park

Rocky Mountain National Park

Downtown River Walk

Open Air Adventure Park

Fun City

Mini-Golf

Fishing

Mountain School

Hiking

Guided Tours

Horseback Riding

The Stanley Hotel

Aerial Tram

YMCA

Inspired Artisan Market & Studio

Trolley Tours

The Rock Inn Mountain Tavern & Inn on Fall River for Live Music

Lake Estes Marina

Peak to Peak Scenic by-way

Rafting

Estes Park Museum

Kent Mountain Adventure Center

MacGregor Ranch Museum

Historic Park Theatre & Cafe

Estes Park Memorial Observatory

George Hix Riverside Plaza

Lake Estes

Beaver Meadows Visitor Center

Some activities are seasonal

ESTES PARK

Banana Pancakes

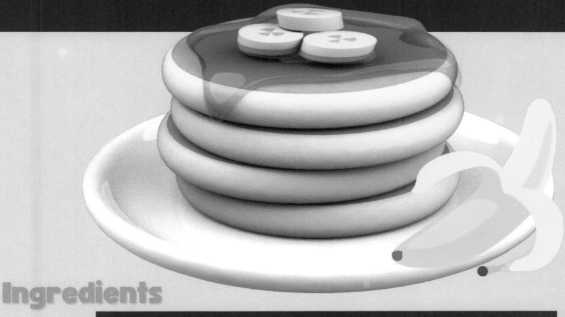

Ingredients

½ cup old-fashioned oatmeal
¾ cup almond milk
½ cup almond flour
1 ripe banana
2 tablespoons white sugar
1 teaspoon vanilla extract
½ teaspoon ground cinnamon
½ teaspoon baking powder
¼ teaspoon salt

Instructions:

Blend oats in a blender until it becomes a fine powder. Add ingredients and blend until well mixed. Let batter sit until thickened, about 10 minutes.

Heat a skillet over medium-high heat and coat with cooking spray. Drop 1/4 cup batter onto the hot skillet and cook until bubbles form and edges are dry, 3 to 4 minutes. Flip and cook until browned on the other side, 2 to 3 minutes. Repeat with remaining batter.

"THE QUIETER YOU BECOME
THE MORE YOU CAN HEAR."

Ram Dass

RIVER
OTTER

RIVER OTTERS ARE SEMIAQUATIC ANIMALS LIKE BEAVERS AND MUSKRATS. THEY LIVE IN BOTH FRESHWATER AND SALTWATER AND ARE ON THE ENDANGERED SPECIES LIST. THEY HAVE SHORT LEGS AND WEBBED FEET THAT HELP THEM SWIM, AND THEIR LONG, NARROW BODIES, FLAT HEADS AND LONG, STRONG TAILS HELP THEM MANEUVER EFFORTLESSLY IN THE WATER. THEY EVEN HAVE EYES AND EARS TOWARD THE TOP OF THEIR HEAD TO HELP THEM WHEN SWIMMING AT THE WATER'S SURFACE. THEY HAVE AN EXTRA EYELID THAT PROTECTS THEIR EYES WHEN UNDERWATER AND ALLOWS THEM TO SEE WHEN SUBMERGED. THEY CAN STAY UNDERWATER FOR AS LONG AS 8 MINUTES AT A TIME. THEY ARE FAST SWIMMERS, TRAVELING THROUGH THE WATER AT SPEEDS OF UP TO 8 MPH. THEY CAN ALSO DIVE UP TO 60 FEET DEEP. THEIR SHORT, THICK FUR HELPS KEEP THEM WARM WHILE IN COLD WATER. GROUPS ARE OFTEN SEEN SLIPPING AND SLIDING OVER MUDDY OR SNOWY GROUND AND PLAYING AROUND IN WATER. THEIR PLAY HAS A PURPOSE. IT HELPS THE OTTERS LEARN IMPORTANT SURVIVAL SKILLS SUCH AS HUNTING, HOW TO MARK THEIR TERRITORY WITH THEIR SCENT, AND HOW TO DEVELOP SOCIAL BONDS. RIVER OTTERS EAT FISH, CRUSTACEANS, BIRDS, SMALL SNAKES AND CAIMANS. THE MALE OTTER IS CALLED A BOAR WHILE THE FEMALE IS CALLED A SOW. A BABY OTTER IS CALLED A PUP OR A KITTEN. UNLIKE THE SEA OTTER, RIVER OTTERS PREFER TO SLEEP ON LAND IN UNDERGROUND DENS OR SHELTERS.

RIVER
OTTER

MAGPIE

MAGPIES ARE LARGE BIRDS IN THE CROW FAMILY. THEY ARE OMNIVOROUS, WHICH MEANS THEY ARE HERBIVORES (EATS PLANTS), AND CARNIVORES (EATS MEAT) AT THE SAME TIME. THEY FEAST ON INSECTS, MICE, AMPHIBIANS, CARRION, FRUIT, SEEDS, AND MUSHROOMS. THEY ARE KNOWN TO STEAL EGGS OR BABY BIRDS FROM OTHER NESTS. THEY ARE SOMETIMES CALLED BIRD KILLERS BECAUSE OF THIS BEHAVIOR. MAGPIES ARE BEAUTIFUL BIRDS. THEY HAVE BLACK AND WHITE FEATHERS THAT HAVE A GORGEOUS METALLIC SHINE IN BLUE, PURPLE, OR GREEN. THESE GUYS ARE VERY SMART. THEY CAN RECOGNIZE THEMSELVES IN MIRRORS AND HAVE BEEN OBSERVED COUNTING. IN THE MIDDLE AGES, THE MAGPIE WAS ASSOCIATED WITH WITCHES. FOR GERMANS, THE MAGPIE WAS THE BIRD OF HEL, THE GODDESS OF THE DEAD. IN ASIA, THE MAGPIE IS CONSIDERED TO BE GOOD LUCK. NATIVE AMERICANS ALSO THINK HIGHLY OF THE MAGPIE AND BELIEVE IT IS A KIND OF SPIRITUAL BEING.

MAGPIE

Good luck? Bad Luck? Who knows?

An old farmer had a beloved horse who helped the family earn a living. One day, the horse ran away, and their neighbors exclaimed, "Your horse ran away, what terrible fortune!" The farmer replied, "Maybe so, maybe not."

A few days later, the horse retuned home, leading a few wild horses back to the farm as well. The neighbors shouted out, "Your horse has returned, and brought several horses home with him. What great fortune!" The farmer replied, "Maybe so, maybe not."

Later that week, the farmer's son was trying to break one of the horses and she threw him to the ground, breaking his leg. The neighbors cried, "Your son broke his leg, what terrible luck!" The farmer replied, "Maybe so, maybe not."

A few weeks later, soldiers from the national army marched through town, recruiting all boys for the army. They did not take the farmer's son, because of his broken leg. The neighbors shouted, "Your boy is spared, what a tremendous blessing!" To which the farmer replied, "Maybe so, maybe not. We'll see."

The moral of the story is: No event can truly be judged as good or bad, fortunate or unfortunate, lucky or unlucky, but that only time will tell the whole story. (And don't pay attention to nosy neighbors!)

Try to teach yourself how to not look at life experiences as good or bad. Practice calmness and understanding that all things change.

TWO WOLVES

ONE EVENING AN OLD CHEROKEE TOLD HIS GRANDSON ABOUT A BATTLE THAT GOES ON INSIDE PEOPLE. HE SAID:

"MY SON, THE BATTLE IS BETWEEN TWO 'WOLVES' INSIDE US ALL.

ONE IS EVIL. IT IS ANGER, ENVY, JEALOUSY, SORROW, REGRET, GREED, ARROGANCE, SELF-PITY, GUILT, RESENTMENT, INFERIORITY, LIES, FALSE PRIDE, SUPERIORITY, AND EGO.

THE OTHER IS GOOD. IT IS JOY, PEACE, LOVE, HOPE, SERENITY, HUMILITY, KINDNESS, BENEVOLENCE, EMPATHY, GENEROSITY, TRUTH, COMPASSION, AND FAITH."

THE GRANDSON THOUGHT ABOUT IT FOR A MINUTE AND THEN ASKED HIS GRANDFATHER,
"WHICH WOLF WINS?"
THE OLD CHEROKEE SIMPLY REPLIED,
"THE ONE YOU FEED."

MORAL OF THE STORY:

Do not waste your time thinking about the negative, the ugly, the bad. Spend time on the positive, the beauty, the good.

WHY PRACTICE DEEP BREATHING?

The benefits of deep breathing will improve your life in many different ways. Practicing daily will bring changes to your life that will help you for a lifetime.

Releases tension

Eases pain

Releases toxins

Improves mood

Improves blood

Calms the mind

Lion's Breath

SPREAD YOUR FINGERS AS
WIDE AS POSSIBLE.
INHALE THROUGH YOUR NOSE.
OPEN YOUR MOUTH WIDE,
STICK OUT YOUR TONGUE,
& POINT IT DOWN TOWARD
YOUR CHIN.
EXHALE FORCEFULLY, MAKING A
"HA" SOUND THAT COMES FROM
DEEP WITHIN YOUR BELLY.
BREATHE NORMALLY FOR A
FEW MOMENTS.
REPEAT.

*Try to do this for 10 minutes.
If you can't, at least you tried &
can try again tomorrow.*

Bee Breath

SIT IN A COMFORTABLE POSITION.
RAISE YOUR SHOULDERS UP TO YOUR EARS,
THEN RELAX THEM & LET THEM FALL
NATURALLY.
CLOSE YOUR EYES & IMAGINE RELAXATION
MELTING ALL OVER YOU.
SPEND A FEW SECONDS FOCUSING ON EVERY
MAJOR AREA OF YOUR BODY, FROM HEAD
TO TOE, & GENTLY RELAXING EACH PART.
INHALE AS DEEP AS YOU CAN.
EXHALE SLOWLY THROUGH YOUR NOSE.
HUM WHILE EXHALING UNTIL ALL YOUR
BREATH HAS BEEN RELEASED.

Try to do this for 10 minutes.
If you can't, at least you tried &
can try again tomorrow.

Honorable Mention

Snowshoe Hare - The snowshoe hare is one of the most common forest mammals but is found only in North America.

Raven - Though a group of ravens is called an unkindness, ravens often show empathy towards other birds.

Turkey - A male's poop is shaped like the letter J and the female's is more spiral-shaped.

Coyote - Coyotes are the most vocal wild mammals in North America. They make 11 different sounds: growl, huff, woof, bark, bark-howl, lone howl, group yip-howl, whine, group howl, greeting songs, and yelps.

Bobcat - They are excellent swimmers, climbers, and runners. They can run up to 30 MPH.

Bald Eagle - Nests have been found that are as deep as 13 feet, up to 8 feet wide, and can weigh as much as 2000 pounds!

Red-tailed Hawk -Their eyesight is 8 times as powerful as a human's.

DON'T GIVE UP 5 MINUTES BEFORE THE BLESSING!

River

Stanley Hotel

Fall River

THE
INN ON FALL RIVER
CABINS
FIREPLACES
HOT TUB
TONIGHT 8:00 PM

VACANCY

Estes Park

Fall River

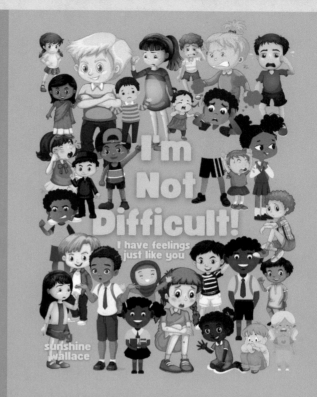

THE HELPFUL COLLECTION

Sunshine Wallace, LLC 2022
SunshineWallace222@gmail.com

You've got this!

CPSIA information can be obtained
at www.ICGtesting.com
Printed in the USA
BVHW021319090522
636522BV00002B/13